CANADA

R.L. Van

Big Buddy Books
An Imprint of Abdo Publishing
abdobooks.com

abdobooks.com

Published by Abdo Publishing, a division of ABDO, PO Box 398166, Minneapolis, Minnesota 55439. Copyright © 2023 by Abdo Consulting Group, Inc. International copyrights reserved in all countries. No part of this book may be reproduced in any form without written permission from the publisher. Big Buddy Books™ is a trademark and logo of Abdo Publishing.

Printed in the United States of America, North Mankato, Minnesota
102022
012023

THIS BOOK CONTAINS RECYCLED MATERIALS

Design: Emily O'Malley, Mighty Media, Inc.
Production: Mighty Media, Inc.
Editor: Jessica Rusick
Cover Photograph: kavram/Shutterstock Images
Interior Photographs: AlexAranda/Shutterstock Images, p. 29 (bottom); alexsl/iStockphoto, p. 30 (flag); Andrea Izzotti/Shutterstock Images, p. 27 (top left); ANGELA WEISS/Getty Images, p. 23; benedek/iStockphoto, p. 6 (middle); Birdiegal/Shutterstock Images, p. 28; dbarcroft/iStockphoto, p. 30 (currency); Denys/iStockphoto, p. 7 (map); Elena Elisseeva/Shutterstock Images, p. 15; EQRoy/Shutterstock Images, p. 26 (left); ImagineGolf/iStockphoto, p. 17; LauriPatterson/iStockphoto, p. 19; lucky-photographer/iStockphoto, p. 25; lukulo/iStockphoto, pp. 5 (compass), 7 (compass); macri roland/Shutterstock Images, p. 21; MarinaDa/Shutterstock Images, p. 13; MJ_Prototype/iStockphoto, p. 26 (right); Pgiam/iStockphoto, p. 6 (top); Pyty/Shutterstock Images, p. 5 (map); R.M. Nunes/iStockphoto, p. 6 (bottom); Ryan Remiorz/AP Images, p. 27 (top right); Science History Images/Alamy Photo, p. 9; Sean Kilpatrick/AP Images, p. 29 (top); Sergei Bachlakov/Shutterstock Images, p. 11; steve estvanik/Shutterstock Images, p. 27 (bottom)
Design Elements: Mighty Media, Inc.
Country population and area figures taken from the CIA World Factbook

Library of Congress Control Number: 2022940520

Publisher's Cataloging-in-Publication Data
Names: Van, R.L., author.
Title: Canada / by R.L. Van
Description: Minneapolis, Minnesota : Abdo Publishing, 2023 | Series: Countries | Includes online resources and index.
Identifiers: ISBN 9781532199561 (lib. bdg.) | ISBN 9781098274764 (ebook)
Subjects: LCSH: Canada--Juvenile literature. | North America--Juvenile literature. | Canada--History--Juvenile literature. | Geography--Juvenile literature.
Classification: DDC 971--dc23

CONTENTS

PASSPORT TO CANADA

Canada is a North American country. It is split into **provinces** and **territories**. It is the world's second-largest country by area. More than 38 million people live there.

WHERE IS CANADA?
N
W
E
S
Arctic Ocean
Greenland
CANADA
Atlantic Ocean
United States

IMPORTANT CITIES

Ottawa is Canada's **capital** and fourth-largest city. It is known for education and its historic sites.

Toronto is Canada's largest city. It is one of the most multicultural cities in the world. It is also a center of business.

Montreal is Canada's second-largest city. It is known for airplane manufacturing and its culture.

SAY IT

Ottawa
AH-tuh-wuh

Toronto
tuh-RAHN-toh

Montreal
mahn-tree-AWL

DID YOU KNOW?

More than half of the people in Montreal speak French at home.

CANADA IN HISTORY

First Nations people were the first people to live in Canada. Their ancestors crossed a land bridge between Asia and North America.

When Europeans arrived, they discovered Canada's **natural resources**. The French settled there in the 1600s to trade furs.

First Nations people traded furs to the French for metal and cloth.

In 1763, Great Britain took control of Canada. In 1867, Canada formed its own government. People worked to grow the country's businesses. Today, the government works hard to ensure its **provinces** and **territories** stay **united**.

Canada Day is July 1. It celebrates the formation of Canada's government.

AN IMPORTANT SYMBOL

Canada's flag is red and white. Its maple leaf represents Canadian pride. Canada is a **federal parliamentary democracy**. A prime minister leads the government. A governor general represents the **United** Kingdom's king or queen. These two parts make laws together.

Canada's flag was
adopted in 1965.

ACROSS THE LAND

Canada is known for its beauty. Mountains, forests, and **tundra** cover the land. Moose, bears, beavers, and more live in Canada. Whales swim in the coastal waters. Canada's plants include trees, mosses, and grasses.

Canada has hundreds of
bodies of water, including
the Great Lakes.

EARNING A LIVING

Many Canadians work in health care, education, and sales. Factory workers make cars and machinery.

Canada has many **natural resources**. These include lumber and gold. Farmers produce grains, meats, and dairy. Fish and lobster come from Canada's waters.

Canada is one of
the world's largest
producers of lumber.

LIFE IN CANADA

Canada is influenced by French, British, American, and **Indigenous** cultures. Poutine is a famous dish. Canada's maple syrup is famous too. Ice hockey and lacrosse are Canada's national sports. Baseball and Canadian football are also popular.

Poutine is French fries
and cheese curds topped
with brown gravy.

FAMOUS FACES

Autumn Peltier is a youth activist from the Wiikwemkoong First Nation in Ontario. Since 2016, she has been fighting for clean drinking water in **Indigenous** communities. Peltier has won national and international awards for her work.

Autumn Peltier has been nominated for the International Children's Peace Prize three times.

Justin Bieber was born in Ontario. In 2007, he and his mom began to post videos of him singing on YouTube. Bieber's first album came out in 2009. Since then, he has made many more albums. Bieber has also won two Grammy Awards.

Justin Bieber is one of the best-selling musicians of all time.

A GREAT COUNTRY

Canada is known for its beautiful landscapes and welcoming community. Its people and places help make the world a more interesting place.

DID YOU KNOW?

Many American movies are made in Canada because it is cheaper to film there.

Banff National Park was founded in 1885.
It is the oldest national park in Canada.

TOUR BOOK

If you ever visit Canada, here are some places to go and things to do!

EXPLORE

Visit the Bata Shoe Museum in Toronto. It has more than 14,000 footwear-related artifacts!

HIKE

Hike past glaciers, lakes, and wildlife at Jasper National Park in Alberta.

Visit Vancouver's Stanley Park. Learn about the park's **Indigenous** history and art.

Watch the Montreal Canadiens play hockey. The team has won more Stanley Cups than any other **NHL** team.

In July, attend the Calgary Stampede. This world-famous rodeo has live music, a dog show, rides, and more.

TIMELINE

1873

The Canadian government formed the Northwest Mounted Police.

1980

The song "O Canada" became Canada's national anthem.

1497

John Cabot discovered Canada's rich fishing areas, leading to more European exploration of Canada.

1993

The Montreal Canadiens hockey team won its twenty-fourth Stanley Cup.

2021

Mary Simon became the first **Indigenous** Canadian governor general.

1982

Canada became a fully independent country.

2010

Canada won the most gold medals at the Winter Olympics in Vancouver.

CANADA
UP CLOSE

Official Name
Canada

Flag

Population
38,232,593 (2022 est.)
38th-most-populated country

Total Area
3,855,103 square miles
(9,984,670 sq km)
2nd-largest country

Official Languages
English, French

Capital
Ottawa

Currency
Canadian dollar

National Anthem
"O Canada"

Form of Government
Federal parliamentary
democracy under
a constitutional
monarchy

GLOSSARY

capital—a city where government leaders meet.

federal parliamentary democracy—a government in which people elect representatives to parliament, and these representatives choose a leader. The central government and the individual states and territories share power.

Indigenous—of or relating to ethnic groups descended from the first people known to live in a certain place.

natural resources—useful and valuable supplies from nature.

NHL—National Hockey League. The NHL is a group of ice hockey teams in the United States and Canada.

province—a large section within a country, like a state.

territory—an area that is not a province but is under the authority of a country's government.

tundra—flat, frozen Arctic land with no trees.

united—joined together for a purpose or action.

ONLINE RESOURCES

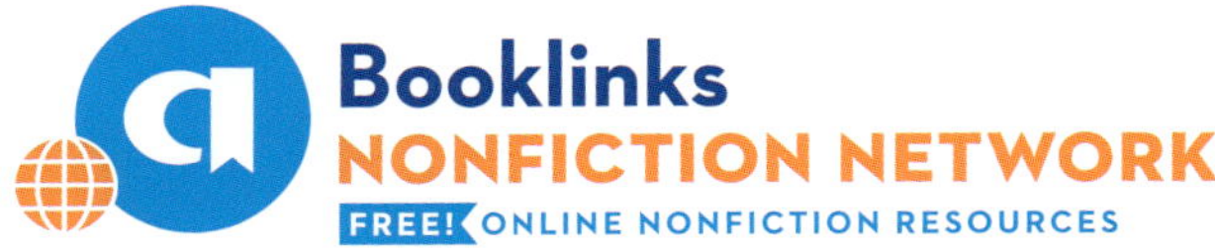

To learn more about Canada, please visit **abdobooklinks.com** or scan this QR code. These links are routinely monitored and updated to provide the most current information available.

INDEX